Presented to:

_____

From:

_____

Date:

_____

JESUS
THE REASON FOR THE SEASON

Honor Books

Tulsa, Oklahoma

Jesus: The Reason for the Season
ISBN 1-56292-938-0
Copyright © 2001 by Honor Books
P.O. Box 55388
Tulsa, Oklahoma 74155

Second printing

INTRODUCTION

The Christmas season often brings with it a renewed desire to simplify our lives and lay hold of those things that are truly important. As we sing familiar carols about peace on earth and silent nights, we find ourselves longing for simple pleasures, tranquility, and purpose.

As you watch another Christmas season unfold, we hope that you will let the prayers, hymns, poems, scriptures, and inspirational quotes included in this little book remind you that Jesus truly is the reason for this joyous season. We hope you will be inspired as you follow the events of the first Christmas, complete with angels and emperors, shepherds and wise men, prophets and priests. We pray that your heart will be transformed as you read about the humble couple who kept watch over the holy Infant in a manger bed.

Let the inspiring words you find in these pages bring you joy, comfort, and peace as you refocus and remember—Jesus is the Reason for the Season.

CONTENTS

PILGRIM'S PRAYER

May the Babe of Bethlehem be yours to tend;
May the Boy of Nazareth be yours for friend;
May the Man of Galilee His healing send;
May the Christ of Calvary His courage lend;
May the risen Lord His presence send;
And His holy angels defend you to the end.

Jesus

THE BABE OF BETHLEHEM

CHRISTMAS LEXICON

Nativity: Christmas Day, the anniversary of the birth of Jesus.

The Cave of the Nativity is under the chancel of the Church of the Nativity. In the recess, a few feet above the ground, is a stone slab with a star cut into it to mark the spot where the Savior was born. Near it is a hollow scarped out of the rock, said to be the place where the infant Jesus was laid.

—E. COBHAM BREWER

CHRISTMAS IN BETHLEHEM

The ancient dream: a cold, clear night made brilliant by a glorious star, the smell of incense, shepherds and wise men falling to their knees in adoration of the sweet baby, the incarnation of perfect love.

—LUCINDA FRANKS

JOSEPH'S STORY

*These are the facts concerning
the birth of Jesus Christ:
His mother, Mary, was engaged to be married
to Joseph. But while she was still a virgin
she became pregnant by the Holy Spirit.*

*Then Joseph, her fiancé, being a man of stern
principle, decided to break the engagement but to do
it quietly, as he didn't want to publicly disgrace her.*

As he lay awake considering this, he fell into a dream,
and saw an angel standing beside him,
"Joseph, son of David," the angel said,
"don't hesitate to take Mary as your wife!
For the child within her has been conceived by the Holy Spirit.
And she will have a Son, and you
shall name him Jesus (meaning 'Savior'),
for he will save his people from their sins. . . . "

When Joseph awoke, he did as the angel commanded
and brought Mary home to be his wife.

MATTHEW 1:18-21,24 TLB

*L*ove came down at Christmas,
Love all lovely, Love Divine;
Love was born at Christmas;
Star and angels gave the sign.

—CHRISTINA ROSSETTI

*All my heart this night rejoices
As I hear, far and near,
Sweetest angel voices.
"Christ is born,"
Their choirs are singing,
Till the air everywhere
Now with joy is ringing.*

—PAUL GERHARDT

THE TRIP TO BETHLEHEM

Caesar Augustus, the Roman emperor, decreed that a census should be taken throughout the nation. . . .
Everyone was required to return to his ancestral home for this registration.

*Because Joseph was a
member of the royal line,
he had to go to Bethlehem in Judea,
King David's ancient home—
journeying there from the
Galilean village of Nazareth.*

LUKE 2:1,3-4 TLB

Great as he was, Caesar Augustus is now only an echo of ancient times, while the name of the Child he had never heard of is spoken by millions with reverence and love.

—WALTER RUSSELL BOWIE

MARY'S STORY

He took with him Mary, his fiancée,
who was obviously pregnant by this time.
And while they were there, the time
came for her baby to be born;
and she gave birth to her first child, a son.
She wrapped him in a blanket and
laid him in a manger,
because there was no room
for them in the village inn.

LUKE 2:5-7 TLB

O LITTLE TOWN OF BETHLEHEM

For Christ is born of Mary,
and gathered all above,
while mortals sleep, the angels keep
their watch of wondering love.

O Morning Stars, together,
proclaim the holy birth,
and praises sing to God the King,
and peace to all on earth!

O holy Child of Bethlehem!
Descend to us, we pray;
cast out our sin, and enter in,
be born in us today!

We hear the Christmas angels
the great glad tidings tell;
O come to us, abide with us,
our Lord Immanuel!

—PHILLIPS BROOKS

The hinge of history is on the door
of a Bethlehem stable.

—RALPH W. SOCKMAN

*I*nfant holy, Infant lowly,
for his bed a cattle stall;
oxen lowing, little knowing,
Christ the Babe is Lord of all.
Swift are winging angels singing,
noels ringing, tidings bringing;
Christ the Babe is Lord of all.[1]

—POLISH CAROL,
ENGLISH TRANSLATION BY
EDITH M.G. REED

Given, not lent,
And not withdrawn, once sent,
This Infant of mankind, this One,
Is still the little welcome Son.

New every year,
Newborn and newly dear,
He comes with tidings and a song,
The ages long, the ages long.

Even as the cold
Keen winter grows not old,
As childhood is so fresh, foreseen,
And spring in the familiar green.

Sudden as sweet
Come the expected feet.
All joy is young, and new all art,
And He, too, whom we have by heart.

—ALICE MEYNELL

*"The virgin will be with child
and will give birth to a son,
and they will call him
Immanuel"—which means,
"God with us."*

MATTHEW 1:23

GOD WITH US

*T*hat's what Immanuel means. The prophet Isaiah foretold Jesus' birth and said He would be called Immanuel and Wonderful Counselor, Mighty God, Everlasting Father, Prince of Peace.

No longer would we walk through life alone with God watching us from a distance; Jesus' birth, life, death, and resurrection eliminated the barrier of sin and death and brought God to us—and us to God.

In our darkest hours, in our saddest moments, when fear and violence and loneliness seem to rule the planet, let us take comfort that we are not alone. Immanuel. God with us.

—ROSE GALLION

*I*t is a high article to believe that
this infant, born of Mary, is true God;
for nobody's reason can ever accept
the fact that he who created heaven and earth
and is adored by the angels was born of a virgin.
That is the article. Nobody believes it
except he who also knows this faith,
namely, that this child is the Lord and Savior.

—MARTIN LUTHER

The Lord's promise came true,
just as the prophet had said,
"A virgin will have a baby boy,
and he will be called Immanuel,"
which means "God is with us."

MATTHEW 1:22-23 CEV

CHRIST'S NATIVITY

Awake, glad heart! get up and sing!
It is the birth-day of thy King.
Awake! awake!
The Sun doth shake
Light from his locks, and all the way
Breathing perfumes, doth spice the day.

I would I had in my best part
Fit rooms for thee! or that my heart
Were so clean as Thy manger was!
But I am all filth, and obscene;
Yet, if thou wilt, thou canst make clean.

Sweet Jesus! will then. Let no more
This leper haunt and soil Thy door!
Cure him, ease him, O release him!
And let once more, by mystic birth,
The Lord of life be born in earth.

—HENRY VAUGHN

THE FRIENDLY BEASTS

Jesus, our brother, kind and good,
Was humbly born in a stable rude.
And the friendly beasts around Him stood,
Jesus, our brother, kind and good.

"I," said the donkey, shaggy and brown,
"I carried His mother uphill and down;
I carried her safely to Bethlehem town;
I," said the donkey, shaggy and brown.

"I," said the cow all white and red,
"I gave Him my manger for His bed;
I gave Him my hay to pillow His head;
I," said the cow all white and red.

"I," said the sheep with the curly horn,
"I gave Him my wool for His blanket warm;
He wore my coat on Christmas morn;
I," said the sheep with the curly horn.

"I," said the dove from the rafters high,
"Cooed Him to sleep, my mate and I;
We cooed Him to sleep my mate and I;
I," said the dove from the rafters high.

And every beast by some good spell
In the stable dark was glad to tell
Of the gift he gave Immanuel,
The gift he gave Immanuel.

—TWELFTH-CENTURY CAROL

*O*ur first Christmas gift is the Gift of gifts, Jesus himself, the Son of God. Without Christ there is no Christmas, for a Christmas without Christ is meaningless. But the tiny Babe in the crib has conquered all hearts. His birthday has become a day of joy for the whole world.

Jesus

THE NEWBORN KING

THE HARPER'S SONG

Sing glory, glory, glory!
And bless God's holy name;
For 'twas on Christmas morning
The little Jesus came.

He wore no robes. No crown of gold
Was on his head that morn;
But herald angels sang for joy
To tell a King was born.

O glory, glory, glory!
We bless God's holy name;
For 'twas to bring His wondrous love
That little Jesus came.

And in His praise our songs we sing,
And in His name we pray;
God bless us all for Jesus' sake,
This happy Christmas Day.

—MAUD LINDSAY, "THE PROMISE"

CHRISTMAS LEXICON

Angelic Hymn: The hymn beginning with "Glory be to God on high" (Luke 2:14) so called because the former part of it was sung by the angel host that appeared to the shepherds of Bethlehem.

—E. COBHAM BREWER

HARK THE HERALD ANGELS SING

Hark! The herald angels sing,
"Glory to the newborn King;
Peace on earth, and mercy mild—
God and sinners reconciled!"
Joyful, all ye nations rise, join the triumph of the skies;
With angelic hosts proclaim,
"Christ is born in Bethlehem!"
Hark! The herald angels sing,
"Glory to the newborn King!"

—CHARLES WESLEY

THE ANGELS' STORY

*That night some shepherds were
in the fields outside the village,
guarding their flocks of sheep. Suddenly
an angel appeared among them, and the
landscape shone bright with the glory of the Lord.
They were badly frightened, but the angel
reassured them. "Don't be afraid!" he said.
"I bring you the most joyful news ever announced,
and it is for everyone! The Savior—yes, the Messiah,
the Lord—has been born tonight in Bethlehem!*

How will you recognize him?

You will find a baby wrapped in a blanket, lying in a manger!"

Suddenly, the angel was joined by a vast host of others—the armies of heaven—praising God: "Glory to God in the highest heaven," they sang, "and peace on earth for all those pleasing him."

LUKE 2:8-14 TLB

ANGELS FROM THE REALMS OF GLORY

Angels from the realms of glory,
wing your flight o'er all the earth;
ye who sang creation's story,
now proclaim Messiah's birth:

Shepherds, in the field abiding,
watching o'er your flocks by night,
God with us is now residing;
yonder shines the infant light:

Come and worship, come and worship,
worship Christ, the newborn king.

—JAMES MONTGOMERY

What sweeter music can we bring
  Than a carol, for to sing
The birth of this our Heavenly King?
Awake the voice! awake the string!
Heart, ear, and eye, and everything,
Awake! the while the active finger
  Runs division with the singer.

—ROBERT HERRICK

*Y*e heavenly choir
Assist me to sing
And strike the soft lyre,
And honour our king:

His mighty salvation
Demands all our praise,
Our best adoration,
And loftiest lays.

All glory to God,
Who ruleth on high,
And now hath bestowed,
And sent from the sky

Christ Jesus the Saviour;
Poor mortals to bless:
The pledge of his favour,
the seal of his peace.

—CHARLES WESLEY

THE SHEPHERDS' STORY

When this great army of angels had returned again to heaven, the shepherds said to each other, "Come on! Let's go to Bethlehem! Let's see this wonderful thing that has happened, which the Lord has told us about."

They ran to the village and found their way to Mary and Joseph. And there was the baby, lying in the manger. The

shepherds told everyone what had happened and what the angel had said to them about this child. . . .

*Then the shepherds went back again to their
fields and flocks,
praising God for the visit of the angels,
and because they had seen the child,
just as the angel had told them.*

LUKE 2:15-17,20 TLB

*F*locks were sleeping, shepherds keeping
vigil till the morning new
saw the glory, heard the story,
tidings of a gospel true.
Thus rejoicing, free from sorrow,
praises voicing, greet the morrow:
Christ the babe was born for you.[1]

—POLISH CAROL, ENGLISH TRANSLATION BY EDITH M.G. REED

It isn't far to Bethlehem town,
It's anywhere that Christ comes down,
And feels in people's smiling face,
A loving and abiding place.
The road to Bethle'm runs right through
The homes of folks like me and you.

But when to Bethlehem they came,
Whereas this infant lay;
They found him in a manger
Where oxen feed on hay,
His mother Mary kneeling
Unto the Lord did pray.
O tidings of comfort and joy,
Jesus Christ our Saviour was
born on Christmas day.

Now to the Lord sing praises,
All you within this place,
And with true love and brotherhood
Each other now embrace;
This holy tide of Christmas
All others doth deface.
O tidings of comfort and joy,
Jesus Christ our Saviour
was born on Christmas day.

—UNKNOWN

CHRISTMAS LEXICON

Noël: Christmas day, or a Christmas carol. A contraction of *nouvelles* (tidings), written in old English, *nowells.*

—E. COBHAM BREWER

OLD CAROL

A child this day is born,
A child of high renown,
Most worthy of a sceptre,
A sceptre and a crown.
Nowells, nowells, nowells!
Sing all we may,
Because that Christ, the King,
Was born this blessed day.

Come worship the King,
That little dear thing,
Asleep on His Mother's soft breast.
Ye bright stars, bow down,
Weave for Him a crown,
Christ Jesus by angels confessed.

Come, children, and peep,
But hush ye, and creep
On tiptoe to where the Babe lies;
Then whisper His Name
And lo! like a flame
The glory light shines
in His eyes.

Come, strong men, and see
This high mystery,
Tread firm where the shepherds have trod,
And watch, 'mid the hair
Of the Maiden so fair,
The five little fingers of God.

Come, old men and grey,
The star leads the way,
It halts and your wanderings cease;
Look down on His Face
Then, filled with His Grace,
Depart ye, God's servants, in Peace.

—G.A. STUDDERT KENNEDY

*In the pure soul, whether it sing or pray,
The Christ is born anew from day to day.
The life that knoweth Him shall bide apart
And keep eternal Christmas in the heart.*

—ELIZABETH STUART PHELPS

*B*e so in tune with the exultant song of the angels during this Christmas season that others may see and hear that Christ dwells with you.

SIMEON'S STORY

*Eight days later, at the baby's circumcision
ceremony, he was named Jesus, the name given
him by the angel before he was even conceived. . . .
That day a man named Simeon, a Jerusalem resident,
was in the Temple. He was a good man,
very devout, filled with the Holy Spirit and
constantly expecting the Messiah to come soon.*

For the Holy Spirit had revealed to him that he would not die until he had seen him— God's anointed King. . . .

Simeon . . . took the child in his arms, praising God. "Lord," he said, "now I can die content! For I have seen him as you promised me I would. I have seen the Savior you have given to the world. He is the Light that will shine upon the nations, and he will be the glory of your people Israel!"

LUKE 2:21,25-26,28-32 TLB

They were all looking for a king
To slay their foes, and lift them high;
Thou cam'st, a little baby thing
That made a woman cry.

—GEORGE MACDONALD

"The days are coming," declares the LORD, "when I will raise up to David a righteous Branch, a King who will reign wisely and do what is just and right in the land."

JEREMIAH 23:5

Compassionate and holy God,
We celebrate with joy
Your coming into our midst;
We celebrate with hope
Your coming into our midst;
We celebrate with peace
Your coming into our midst;
For You have come to save us.
By Your grace we recognize
Your presence in men and women
In all parts of Your world . . .

Through Your strength our
lives can proclaim joy and hope;
Through Your love we can work for peace and justice.
You are the Source of our being;
You are the Light of our lives.

—BASED ON LINES FROM
A LATIN-AMERICAN PRAYER

*Jesus came!—and came for me.
Simple words! and yet expressing
Depths of holy mystery,
Depths of wondrous love and blessing.
Holy Spirit, make me see
All His coming means for me;
Take the things of Christ, I pray,
Show them to my heart today.*

—FRANCES RIDLEY HAVERGAL

ANNA'S STORY

*Anna, a prophetess, was also
there in the Temple that day.
She was the daughter of Phanuel,
of the Jewish tribe of Asher, and was very
old. . . . She never left the Temple but
stayed there night and day, worshiping
God by praying and often fasting.*

*She came along just as Simeon
was talking with Mary and Joseph,
and she also began thanking God and
telling everyone in Jerusalem who had
been awaiting the coming of the Savior
that the Messiah had finally arrived.*

LUKE 2:36-38 TLB

OUR SOULS ADORE

The King of glory sends his Son,
To make his entrance on this earth;
Behold the midnight bright as noon,
And heav'nly hosts declare his birth!

About the young Redeemer's head,
What wonders, and what glories meet!
An unknown star arose, and led
The eastern sages to his feet.

Simeon and Anna both conspire
The infant Saviour to proclaim;
Inward they felt the sacred fire,
And bless'd the babe, and own'd his name.

Let pagan hordes blaspheme aloud,
And treat the holy child with scorn;
Our souls adore th' eternal God
Who condescended to be born.

—ISAAC WATTS

Blessed is the season which engages the whole world in a conspiracy of love.

—HAMILTON WRIGHT MABIE

God showed how much he loved us by sending his only Son into the world so that we might have eternal life through him.

1 JOHN 4:9 NLT

Christmas gift suggestions: To your enemy, forgiveness. To an opponent, tolerance. To a friend, your heart. To a customer, service. To all, charity. To every child, a good example. To yourself, respect.

—OREN ARNOLD

*Be kind and merciful, and forgive others,
just as God forgave you because of Christ.*

EPHESIANS 4:32 CEV

*O*God, you have caused this holy night to shine with the brightness of the true Light: Grant that we, who have known the mystery of that Light on earth, may also enjoy him perfectly in heaven; where with you and the Holy Spirit he lives and reigns, one God, in glory everlasting. Amen.

—THE BOOK OF COMMON PRAYER

THE WISE MEN'S STORY

After Jesus was born in Bethlehem in Judea, during the time of King Herod, Magi from the east came to Jerusalem and asked, "Where is the one who has been born king of the Jews? We saw his star in the east and have come to worship him."
. . . Then Herod called the Magi secretly and found out from them the exact time the star had appeared. He sent them to Bethlehem and said,

"Go and make a careful search for the child. As soon as you find him, report to me, so that I too may go and worship him."

*After they had heard the king, they went on their way,
and the star they had seen in the east went ahead of them
until it stopped over the place where the child was. When they
saw the star, they were overjoyed.*

*On coming to the house, they saw the
child with his mother Mary,
and they bowed down and worshiped him.
Then they opened their treasures and presented him with gifts
of gold and of incense and of myrrh.
And having been warned in a dream not to go back to Herod,
they returned to their country by another route.*

MATTHEW 2:1-2, 7-12

CHRISTMAS LEXICON

The Magi: According to one tradition, they were Melchior, Gaspar, and Balthazar, three kings of the East. The first offered gold, the emblem of royalty, to the infant Jesus; the second, frankincense, in token of divinity; and the third, myrrh, in prophetic allusion to the persecution unto death which awaited the "Man of Sorrows."

Melchior means "King of Light."
Gaspar, or Caspar, means "the white one."
Balthazar means "the lord of treasures."

—E. COBHAM BREWER

*T*he three wise men saw the light and followed it.
They are rightly called wise!

*The Light from heaven
came into the world.*

JOHN 3:19 TLB

There's a song in the air! There's a star in the sky!
There's a mother's deep prayer and a baby's low cry!
And the star rains its fire while the beautiful sing,
for the manger of Bethlehem cradles a King!

There's a tumult of joy o'er the wonderful birth,
for the virgin's sweet boy is the Lord of the earth.
Ay! the star rains its fire while the beautiful sing,
for the manger of Bethlehem cradles a King!

In the light of that star lie the ages impearled;
and that song from afar has swept over the world.
Every hearth is aflame, and the beautiful sing
in the homes of the nations that Jesus is King!

We rejoice in the light, and we echo the song
that comes down through the night
from the heavenly throng.
Ay! we shout to the lovely evangel they bring,
and we greet in his cradle our Savior and King!

—JOSIAH G. HOLLAND

WE THREE KINGS OF ORIENT ARE

We three kings of orient are,
Bearing gifts we traverse afar,
Field and fountain, moor and mountain,
Following yonder star.

O, Star of wonder, star of night,
Star with royal beauty bright,
Westward leading, still proceeding,
Guide us to Thy perfect light.

The stars shone bright that Christmas night,
When Jesus lay on His bed of hay.
The shepherds came from far away
To find the place where the Baby lay.
The wise men brought their gifts of love;
Led by the star that shown from above.

—E. WEBSTER

THE BETHLEHEM STAR

*S*oft winds are blowing
O'er Bethlehem town,
Brightly the stars
From Heaven look down.
Quietly the shepherds
Their long vigil keep,
Over their flocks
Of slumbering sheep.

Hark! There's a sound
On the pulsating air,
Music is stealing
From voices somewhere.
And a beautiful light
As a star settles down
O'er a stable that stands
At the edge of the Town!

—UNKNOWN

The Word became flesh and made his dwelling among us.
We have seen his glory, the glory of the One and Only,
who came from the Father,
full of grace and truth.

JOHN 1:14

O Father, may that holy Star
Grow every year more bright,
And send its glorious beam afar
To fill the world with light.

—WILLIAM CULLEN BRYANT

CAROL OF THE BROWN KING

Of the three Wise Men
Who came to the king,
One was a brown man,
So they sing.

Of the three Wise Men
Who followed the star,
One was a brown king
From afar.

They brought fine gifts
Of spices and gold
In jeweled boxes
Of beauty untold.

Unto His humble
Manger they came
And bowed their heads
In Jesus' name.

Three Wise Men,
One dark like me—
Part of His
Nativity.[2]

—LANGSTON HUGHES

WHO WERE THE WISE MEN?

Who were the Wise Men in the long ago?
Not Herod, fearful lest he lose his throne;
Not Pharisees too proud to claim their own;
Not priests and scribes whose province was
to know;
Not money-changers running to and fro;
But three who traveled, weary and alone,
With dauntless faith, because before
them shone
The star that led them to a
manger low.

Who are the Wise Men now, when all is told?
Not men of science; not the great and strong;
Not those whose eager hands pile high the gold;
But those amid the tumult and the throng
Who follow still the Star of Bethlehem.

—B.Y. Williams

*W*ise men still seek Him!

He will reign over the house of Jacob forever;
his kingdom will never end.

LUKE 1:33

O morning stars together
Proclaim the holy birth,
And praises sing to God the King,
And peace to men on earth.

—PHILLIPS BROOKS

CHRISTMAS PRAYER

O God, our loving Father,
Help us rightly to remember the birth of Jesus,
That we may share in the song of the angels,
The gladness of the shepherds,
And the worship of the wise men. . . .

May the Christmas morning make us happy
To be thy children
And the Christmas evening bring us to
our beds with grateful thoughts,
Forgiving and forgiven, for Jesus' sake.

Amen.

—ROBERT LOUIS STEVENSON

*Here's a word you can take
to heart and depend on:
Jesus Christ came into
the world to save sinners.*

1 TIMOTHY 1:15
THE MESSAGE

Jesus

THE SAVIOR OF THE WORLD

The Mother sits by the rough-hewn byre
where her Baby smiles, and the secret fire
shines on her face. Her hand rests by
an iron spike from the wood thrust high.
("The nails in His hands!")

An open chink in the rude, cold shed
lets in the sky, and the Star that led
shepherds and kings pours down its light:
a silver shaft through the frosty night.
("The spear in His side!")

Her hands reach out, as to push away
the cross-crowned hill and the bloody day;
they touch a rough, unyielding wall:
the stable side, of stone piled tall.
("The stone—rolled away!")

—ALESANDER FLANDREAU

The very purpose of Christ's coming into the world was that He might offer up His life as a sacrifice for the sins of men. He came to die. This is the heart of Christmas.

—BILLY GRAHAM

*I*f we open our hearts and embrace Him . . . not only to reap abundance and joy and health and happy fulfillment, but also the cancellation of our sins—then this is the greatest welcome we can give to the Christ child.

—NORMAN VINCENT PEALE

He brought peace on earth and wants
to bring it also into your soul—
that peace which the world cannot give.
He is the One who would save
His people from their sins.

—CORRIE TEN BOOM

AND THE WORD WAS MADE FLESH

Light looked down and beheld Darkness.
"Thither will I go," said Light.
Peace looked down and beheld War.
"Thither will I go," said Peace.
Love looked down and saw Hatred.
"Thither will I go," said Love.
So came Light and shone.
So came Peace and gave rest.
So came Love and brought Life.

—LAURENCE HOUSMAN

COME THOU LONG-EXPECTED JESUS

Come thou long-expected Jesus,
Born to set thy people free,
From our fears and sins release us,
Let us find our rest in thee:
Israel's strength and consolation,
Hope of all the earth thou art,
Dear desire of every nation,
Joy of every longing heart.

Born thy people to deliver,
Born a child and yet a King,
Born to reign in us for ever,
Now thy gracious kingdom bring:
By thy own eternal Spirit,
Rule in all our hearts alone,
By thy all-sufficient merit
Raise us to thy glorious throne.

—CHARLES WESLEY

*A*lmighty God,
You have given Your only begotten Son to take our nature upon Him,
and to be born of a pure virgin:

Grant that we, who have been born again and made Your children by
  adoption and grace,

may daily be renewed by Your Holy Spirit,

through our Lord Jesus Christ,

to whom with You and the same Spirit be honor and glory,

now and forever.

Amen.

—THE BOOK OF COMMON PRAYER

O holy Child of Bethlehem!
Descend to us, we pray;
Cast out our sin, and enter in,
Be born in us today.

—PHILLIPS BROOKS

OBSERVING CHRISTMAS

We want to hold on to the old customs and traditions because they strengthen our family ties, bind us to our friends, make us one with all mankind for whom the child was born, and bring us back again to the God who gave His only begotten Son, that "whosoever believeth in Him should not perish, but have everlasting life."

So we will not "spend" Christmas nor "observe" Christmas. We will "keep" Christmas—keep it as it is in all the loveliness of its ancient traditions.

May we keep it in our hearts, that we may be kept in its hope.

—PETER MARSHALL

Jesus

THE REASON WE CELEBRATE

CHRISTMAS LEXICON

Christmas Day: Old Christmas Day was January 6th. When Gregory XIII reformed the calendar in 1852, he omitted ten days; but when the New Style was adopted in England in 1752, it was necessary to cut off eleven days, which drove back January 6th to December 25th of the previous year. What we now call January 6th in the Old Style would be Christmas Day or December 25th.

—E. COBHAM BREWER

CAROL SINGING

The practice of singing Christmas carols appears to be almost as old as the celebration of the day itself. In the first days of the Church, the bishops sang carols on Christmas Day, recalling the songs sung by the angels at the birth of Christ.

Praise him for his majestic glory,
the glory of his name.

PSALM 29:2 TLB

CHRISTMAS IN ITALY

In Italy, the *Presepio* or *crib* plays a major part in the celebration of Christmas. Every home, even the poorest, has a *Presepio* of some kind, and the churches have very elaborate ones. The people place humble gifts of nuts and apples in the hands of the life-sized figures.

There are different kinds of gifts, but the same Spirit. There are different kinds of service, but the same Lord.

1 CORINTHIANS 12:4-5

CHRISTMAS IN POLAND

It is a Polish custom not to serve Christmas dinner until the evening star has appeared. A vacant chair is always placed at the table to signify that a place has been made for the little Child of Bethlehem.

*"Surely I am with you always,
to the very end of the age."*

MATTHEW 28:20

CHRISTMAS IN SOUTH AMERICA

A touchingly beautiful Christmas custom is observed at early Mass on Christmas morning in some parts of South America. As the Nativity is reenacted, an Indian lullaby is sung to quiet the Christ Child in His cradle of straw. The music of little bells and rattles can be heard as worshippers celebrate the divine birth.

I will lie down in peace and sleep,
for though I am alone, O Lord,
you will keep me safe.

PSALM 4:8 TLB

CHRISTMAS IN EGYPT

In Egypt, Christians burn candles, lamps, and logs in great numbers on Christmas Eve as symbols of the "shepherds' fire."

You will light my lamp;
The LORD my God will
enlighten my darkness.

PSALM 18:28 NKJV

CHRISTMAS IN SERBIA

Well-to-do families in Serbia keep open house for three days at Christmas, and all visitors—friends or enemies, strangers or beggars—are welcome to come to the table.

On Christmas Eve, the Serbians have a saying: "Tonight earth is blended with Paradise."

"When you put on a dinner . . . invite the poor, the crippled, the lame, and the blind. . . . God will reward you for inviting those who can't repay you."

LUKE 14:12-14 TLB

CHRISTMAS IN HAWAII

In Hawaii, Christmas starts with the coming of the *Christmas Tree Ship* bringing a great load of Christmas fare.

They opened their treasures and presented him with gifts of gold and of incense and of myrrh.

MATTHEW 2:11

CHRISTMAS IN INDIA

Christians in India celebrate by decorating mango and banana trees rather than the traditional evergreens. Some houses use mango leaves inside the house, and others line their flat roofs and walls with small clay oil-burning lamps. For Christmas Eve services, churches are decorated with poinsettias and brightly lit candles.

Though I sit in darkness,
the LORD will be my light.

MICAH 7:8

CHRISTMAS IN GERMANY

It was common in the sixteenth century for Christians in Germany to decorate fir trees—both inside and out—with roses, apples, and colored paper.

Coming home one dark winter night near Christmas, Martin Luther, the Protestant reformer, was struck with the beauty of the starlight shining through the branches of a small fir tree. In an effort to duplicate this beautiful sight, he attached candles to the branches of his indoor Christmas tree.

O LORD, our Lord, how majestic is
your name in all the earth!

PSALM 8:9

CHRISTMAS IN GREECE

Christians in Greece bake traditional Christmas cakes, or *kouloures,* which are decorated with a symbol of the family's profession. A coin is baked inside the cake. The oldest member of the family makes the sign of the cross on the bread with a knife, and then parts are broken off—the first for Jesus, another for Mary, and then one for each family member. It is believed that the person whose piece contains the coin will be especially blessed in the upcoming year.

Every good and perfect gift is from above, coming down from the Father.

JAMES 1:17

CHRISTMAS IN BRAZIL

Christmas dinner in Brazil usually consists of pork, chicken, turkey, ham, rice, salad, and fresh and dried fruits. The less fortunate eat chicken and rice to celebrate the birth of the Christ Child.

The LORD gives strength to his people;
the LORD blesses his people with peace.

PSALM 29:11

*C*hristmas, my child, is love in action.
Every time we love, every time we give, it's Christmas.

—DALE EVANS

Jesus

THE REASON WE GIVE

CHRISTMAS LEXICON

Christmas Box: A small gratuity given to servants, etc., on Boxing Day (the day after Christmas Day). In the early days of Christianity, boxes were placed in churches to collect money for various charities, and opened on Christmas Day. The contents were distributed the next day by the priests, and called the "dole of the Christmas box," or the "box money." It was customary for heads of houses to give small sums of money to their subordinates "to put into the box" before mass on Christmas Day.

—E. COBHAM BREWER

*L*ove of our fellow men should prevail over all hatred and bitterness, a time when our thoughts and deeds and the spirit of our lives manifest the presence of God.

—GEORGE F. MCDOUGALL

My dear friends, we must love each other. Love comes from God, and when we love each other, it shows that we have been given new life. We are now God's children, and we know him.

1 JOHN 4:7 CEV

THE MEANING OF CHRISTMAS

In the school we made a special effort to teach our students the meaning of Christmas and to give them lessons in its proper observance.

Not long ago some of our young men spent a holiday in rebuilding a cabin for a helpless coloured woman who is about seventy-five years old. At another time I remember that I made it known in chapel, one night, that a very poor student was suffering from cold because he needed a coat. The next morning two coats were sent to my office for him.

—BOOKER T. WASHINGTON

Christmas is a season of joy and good will,
of singing and merriment,
of generosity and brotherhood.
Christmas is a season of sharing and love.
Christmas is a season of concern for the needs of others,
a season of the helping hand.
And that's as it should be.
For there is great satisfaction in
making others happy.

—SALVATION ARMY WAR CRY

Yes, you will be enriched so that
you can give even more generously.
And when we take your gifts to
those who need them,
they will break out in thanksgiving to God.

2 CORINTHIANS 9:11 NLT

THE CHRISTMAS HEART

The Christmas heart is a beautiful heart for it is full of love and thoughtfulness for others. And the Christmastime heart is a tribute to the most beautiful heart that ever beat.

So let us cherish this Christmas heart and keep it a Christmas heart all through the year to come.

—GEORGE MATTHEW ADAMS

May you have the gladness of Christmas which is hope;
the spirit of Christmas which is peace;
the heart of Christmas which is love.

—ADA V. HENDRICKS

*Mercy, peace and love
be yours in abundance.*

JUDE 1:2

*R*each into your pocket; reach into your heart;
Christmas is the play, and we all play a part.

*The Scriptures say, "Godly people give generously to the poor.
Their good deeds will never be forgotten."*

2 CORINTHIANS 9:9 NLT

WHAT TO GIVE AT CHRISTMAS

Your time: Look for ways to help those who cannot help themselves.

Your love: Give love freely to those who need it most and deserve it least.

Your life: Your life was a gift to you from God; make it a gift from God to others.

Your Lord: Jesus is the greatest Gift of all. Introduce Him to a friend.

Christmas is not a time or a season but a state of mind.
To cherish peace and goodwill, to be plenteous
in mercy, is to have the real spirit of Christmas.
If we think on these things,
there will be born in us a Savior,
and over us all will shine a star,
sending its gleam of hope to the world.

—CALVIN COOLIDGE

his is Christmas—the real meaning of it.
God loving, searching, giving Himself—to us.
Man needing, receiving, giving himself—to God.
Redemption's glorious exchange of gifts!
Without which we cannot live;
Without which we cannot give to
those we love anything of lasting value.
This is the meaning of Christmas—
the wonder and the glory of it.[3]

—RUTH BELL GRAHAM

*S*omehow not only for Christmas
But all the long year through,
The joy that you give to others
Is the joy that comes back to you.
And the more you spend in blessing
The poor and lonely and sad,
The more of your heart's possessing
Returns to make you glad.

—JOHN GREENLEAF WHITTIER

*S*elfishness makes Christmas a burden;
love makes it a delight.

—UNKNOWN

Two marks of a Christian:
giving and forgiving.

*C*hristmas is a time to remember the gift of God's giving nature in every area of life. He gave us the earth on which to live; fellow humans to love and with whom we can work and share; and great meaning in life—to serve others. The gift of God's Son, Jesus, gives us peace to enjoy all these other gifts as His family on earth—and to live in eternal joy. Merry Christmas to us who have received all God's gifts. Joy to the world!

Praise the Lord, the God of Israel, because
he has visited his people and redeemed them.
He has sent us a mighty Savior from
the royal line of his servant David,
just as he promised.

LUKE 1:68-70 NLT

Jesus

THE REASON FOR THE SEASON

*J*esus came, not to hush the natural music of men's lives, nor to fill it with storm and agitation, but to retune every silver chord in that "harp of a thousand strings" and to make it echo with the harmonies of heaven.

—FREDERIC W. FARRAR

Grace, mercy and peace from God the Father and from Jesus Christ, the Father's Son, will be with us in truth and love.

2 JOHN 1:3

*W*e consider Christmas as the encounter, the great encounter, the historical encounter, the decisive encounter, between God and mankind. He who has faith knows this truly; let him rejoice.

—POPE PAUL VI

The LORD says, "Shout and rejoice, O Jerusalem, for I am coming to live among you."

ZECHARIAH 2:10 NLT

*I*t is easy to think Christmas,
and it is easy to believe Christmas,
but it is hard to act Christmas.

You must display a new nature
because you are a new person,
created in God's likeness—
righteous, holy, and true.

EPHESIANS 4:24 NLT

This is Christmas: not the tinsel, not the giving and receiving, not even the carols, but the humble heart that receives anew the wondrous gift, the Christ.

—FRANK MCKIBBEN

He giveth more grace. Wherefore he saith, God resisteth the proud, but giveth grace unto the humble.

JAMES 4:6 KJV

Until one feels the spirit of Christmas,
there is no Christmas.
All else is outward display—
so much tinsel and decorations.
For it isn't the holly; it isn't the snow.
It isn't the tree, not the firelight's glow.
It's the warmth that comes to the hearts of men
when the Christmas spirit returns again.[4]

*Hope does not disappoint us, because
God has poured out his love into our
hearts by the Holy Spirit, whom
he has given us.*

ROMANS 5:5

Take time to be aware that in the very midst of our busy preparations for the celebration of Christ's birth in ancient Bethlehem, Christ is reborn in the Bethlehems of our homes and daily lives. Take time, slow down, be still, be awake to the Divine Mystery that looks so common and so ordinary yet is wondrously present.

—EDWARD HAYS

Be still, and know that I am God: I will be exalted among the heathen, I will be exalted in the earth.

PSALM 46:10 KJV

*O*n Christmas Eve a candle light
To shine abroad through Christmas night,
That those who pass may see its glow,
And walk with Christ a mile or so.

Those who are wise will shine like the brightness of the heavens, and those who lead many to righteousness, like the stars for ever and ever.

DANIEL 12:3

*A*nd Christmas too does ask of us,
To raise our eyes to higher spheres,
Believe the best in life and man,
Embrace new hope, release our fears.

—RICHARD PAUL EVANS

Happy are those who have the God
of Israel as their helper, whose hope
is in the LORD their God.

PSALM 146:5 NLT

*R*ise, happy morn, rise, holy morn,
Draw forth the cheerful day from night;
O Father, touch the East, and light
The light that shone when Hope was born.

—TENNYSON

*The true light that gives light to
every man was coming into the world.*

JOHN 1:9

*Y*ou can never truly enjoy Christmas until you can look up into the Father's face and tell him you have received his Christmas gift.

—JOHN R. RICE

"If you, then, though you are evil, know how to give good gifts to your children, how much more will your Father in heaven give good gifts to those who ask him!"

MATTHEW 7:11

*C*hristmas began in the heart of God.
It is complete only when it reaches the heart of man.

God, who commanded the light to shine
out of darkness, hath shined in our hearts,
to give the light of the knowledge of the
glory of God in the face of Jesus Christ.

2 CORINTHIANS 4:6 KJV

ere is love, that
God sent His Son,
His Son who never offended.
His Son who was always
His delight.

—JOHN BUNYAN

This is my Son, whom I love;
with him I am well pleased.

MATTHEW 3:17

*I*t is Christmas every time you let God love others through you . . . every time you smile at your brother and offer him your hand.

—MOTHER TERESA

"Freely you have received, freely give."

MATTHEW 10:8

*E*verywhere, everywhere Christmas tonight!
For the Christ child who comes is the master of all;
No palace too great—no cottage too small.

—PHILLIPS BROOKS

At the name of Jesus every knee should bow,
of those in heaven, and of those on earth,
and of those under the earth.

PHILIPPIANS 2:10 NKJV

*L*et us keep Christmas beautiful
Without a thought of greed,
That it might live forevermore
To fill our every need,

That it shall not be just a day,
But last a lifetime through,
The miracle of Christmastime
That brings God close to you.

—GARNETT ANN SCHULTZ

*T*his Jesus of Nazareth, without money and arms,
conquered more millions than Alexander,
Caesar, Mohammed, and Napoleon.

—PHILLIP SCHAFF

Peace! Peace! Jesus Christ was born to save.
Calls you one and calls you all
To gain his everlasting hall.

—JOHN M. NEALE

O God,
You make us glad by the yearly festival of the birth
of your only Son Jesus Christ: Grant that we, who
joyfully receive him as our Redeemer,
may with sure confidence behold him when he
comes to be our Judge;
who lives and reigns with you and the Holy Spirit,
one God, now and forever. Amen.

—THE BOOK OF COMMON PRAYER

Whatever else be lost among the years,
Let us keep Christmas still a shining thing;
Whatever doubts assail us, or what fears,
Let us hold close one day, remembering
Its poignant meaning for the hearts of men.
Let us get back our childlike faith again.

—GRACE NOLL CROWELL

*I*f you who have a troubled heart,
listen to the angel's song:
"I bring you tidings of great joy!"
Jesus did not come to condemn you.
If you want to define Christ rightly,
then pay heed to how the angel defines Him:
"A great joy!"

—MARTIN LUTHER

REFERENCES

Unless otherwise indicated, all Scripture quotations are taken from the *Holy Bible, New International Version*®. NIV®. Copyright © 1973, 1978, 1984 by International Bible Society. Used by permission of Zondervan Publishing House. All rights reserved.

Scripture quotations marked KJV are taken from the *King James Version* of the Bible.

Scripture quotations marked NLT are from the *Holy Bible, New Living Translation,* copyright © 1996. Used by permission of Tyndale House Publishers, Inc., Wheaton, Illinois, 60189. All rights reserved.

Scripture quotations marked CEV are from the *Contemporary English Version,* copyright © 1991, 1992, 1995 by the American Bible Society. Used by permission.

Scripture quotations marked THE MESSAGE are taken from *The Message,* copyright © by Eugene H. Peterson, 1993, 1994, 1995, 1996. Used by permission of NavPress Publishing Group.

Verses marked TLB are taken from *The Living Bible* © 1971. Used by permission of Tyndale House Publishers, Inc., Wheaton, Illinois 60189. All rights reserved.

Scripture quotations marked NKJV are taken from *The New King James Version.* Copyright © 1979, 1980, 1982, Thomas Nelson, Inc.

ENDNOTES

[1] (pp. 23,48) Polish carol, English translation by Edith M.G. Reed.

[2] (pp. 84-85) Langston Hughes, "Carol of the Brown King," in *The Book of Christmas* (Pleasantville, NY: Reader's Digest Association, Inc.).

[3] (p. 130) Joan Winmill Brown, *Christmas Joys: A Treasury of Old Favorites and New Gems of Christmas Lore, Legends, and Inspiration* (New York: Doubleday & Company, 1982).

[4] (p. 140) *Encyclopedia of Religious Quotations,* Frank S. Mead, ed., (Grand Rapids, MI: Fleming H. Revell).

Additional copies of this book and other Christmas titles
from Honor Books
are available from your local bookstore.

Christmas Is . . .
The Wonder of Christmas
Merry Christmas
God's Little Christmas Book
Everything I Need to Know about Christmas I Learned from Jesus
Christmas Treasures of the Heart
The Greatest Christmas Ever
The Christmas Cookie Cookbook
The Candymaker's Gift
The Living Nativity

If you have enjoyed this book, or if it has impacted your life,
we would like to hear from you.
Please contact us at:

Honor Books
Department E
P.O. Box 55388
Tulsa, Oklahoma 74155

Or by e-mail at info@honorbooks.com